Winter to Spring

by Carol Pugliano-Martin

Table of Contents

I need to know these words.

birds

chipmunk

fly

2

melt

snow

spring

3

What Does Winter Look Like?

Do you feel the cold air? A new season is here! The new season is winter. Snow covers the ground in some places.

▲ Winter is a cold season.

The weather gets colder in winter.
What clothes do people wear
in winter? People put on warm clothes
to go outside.

◀ Kids have fun
sledding in winter.

5

Some animals go underground.
Some animals go into caves.
These animals stay inside
and sleep until spring.

▲ Chipmunks sleep in winter.
Chipmunks do not eat or drink.

Some animals find a new home in winter. These animals go to a warmer place where they can find food.

▲ Many birds fly a long way to find food.

How Does Winter Change to Spring?

The snow and ice begin to melt. Soon, the days are longer. The weather is warmer, too.

▲ Some birds stay. These birds can live in the cold.

The season changes. Soon, a new season is here. The season is spring!

▲ Spring can be a wet time of year!

What Do Plants Do in Spring?

Do you see the bright colors? Flowers grow in spring. As the days get warmer, plants start to sprout. The grass turns green. Flowers bloom.

 10 ▲ Flowers begin to grow in spring.

Look at the trees! Do you see
the green buds on the branches?
These buds will grow into flowers.

bud

branch

▲ Buds grow on trees in spring.
Buds open and leaves come out.

What Do Animals Do in Spring?

Some birds fly away for winter.
Those birds come back in spring.
Now birds can find plenty of food here.
The birds fill the air with songs.

▲ Birds eat worms and bugs in spring.

Big and little animals look for food.
Animals find more food in this season.

▲ This spider will catch bugs in its web.

Do you see the chipmunk? The chipmunk is awake! It was sleeping all winter.

▲ This chipmunk is ready to eat!

Look for baby animals in spring.

▲ Baby deer are fawns.

Now you can see many colors. Spring is a time when everything wakes up!